POETRY
TO
THE
PEOPLE

Poetry to the People

SELECTED AND EDITED
BY ABBY WENDLE AND SCOTT GREGORY

THIS LAND PRESS

All rights reserved, including right of reproduction
in whole or part in any form.

Select poems appearing in this anthology were originally
published in *THIS LAND* Tulsa, OK. Vincent LoVoi, Publisher;
Michael Mason, Editor.

WWW.THISLANDPRESS.COM

Design by Jeremy Luther
Cover illustration by Audrey Barcus

First Edition, 2013

ISBN-13: 978-1480031852
ISBN-10: 1480031852

CONTENTS

Listen to select poems online at
THISLANDPRESS.COM/P2P
where you see

Preface
Abby Wendle and Scott Gregory ... v

and I got here and began eating

Coming Home
Ken Hada ... 3

the number of heaven and earth
John Colburn ... 4

Ode to the Midwest
Kevin Young ... 11

OG'S AND LEMONADE
Keiyetta Guyon ... 14

Maybe Shawnee
Claire Edwards ... 16

The Middle of Nowhere
Todd Boss ... 18

The Minneapolis Poem
Dobby Gibson ... 21

Driveway
Ron Padgett ... 23

Kaboom Pantoum
Kathy Fagan ... 25

Across the hot shore we walked toward our red hot baby

A Yarn for the Natural State
Steve Healey ... 29

The 500
Richard Stull ... 31

When I was a kid...
Doug Claybourne ... 32

Karma, Oklahoma
Caleb Puckett ... 35

Hard Luck Okie
Roy Turner ... 36

The Stringtown Prison Blues
Stringtown Prison Poetry Workshop ... 38

I tend a stinging nettle patch

Back Roads
Laura Brandenburg ... 43

EMPTY NEXT SYNDROME
Paula Cisewski ... 44

Sowing Ohio
Rochelle Hurt ... 45

Spare Me Yellow Skies
Wilma Elizabeth McDaniel ... 47

Sorry. Sorry. Sorry.
Hannah Brooks-Motl ... 49

its midnight insides are the size of the world

The Ease of Trout
Jeffrey Skemp ... 53

Falling and Rising
John Brehm ... 55

FOX FACE, SNOW FACE
Sun Yung Shin ... 57

Recurrence
Michael White ... 59

Untitled
Jim Moore ... 60

He keeps the ways he's been touched in the pockets of his jacket

Ticket to Ride
Melody Charles ... 63

Rapture
Miss Terri Ford ... 64

Autobiography
Joe Brainard ... 65

Nude in the City
Regina DiPerna ... 66

The Orange Grove Is Beautiful This Time Of Year:
Nick Weaver ... 68

thrtthr whthrrthms
Maria Damon ... 72

In The Field
　Michael Madonick 74
timing
　Odalee Still 75

life goin' on goin' on goin' on

Through a Country
　Joel Stein 81
Jazz on a Diamond-Needle Hi-Fi
　Deborah J. Hunter 83
BULL WHIPPOORWILL
　Merrill Gilfillan 84
Cicada III
　Scott Aycock 85
Cleaning Graves in Calvert
　Quraysh Ali Lansana 86
Cardiology
　Nicklaus Faith 87
Ascension
　Jack Wendle 89

Poets on the Middle of America 91
Acknowledgements 105

Preface

I don't remember her name. I do remember that I interrupted her quiet.

She was a plump, youngish woman, sitting in a folding chair, knitting. Her booth at the small art fair was ready for customers when I walked up and asked if she had time to read a poem.

"What for?" she asked.

The giant headphones around my neck and the fuzzy microphone in my hand gave me away. I didn't just want her to read a poem: I wanted to record, edit and broadcast her voice as part of a podcast. She blushed, then set down her needles and obliged me.

I sat down in the empty folding chair next to hers and handed her a piece of paper with "Cicada III" by Scott Aycock printed on it. She cleared her throat as I inched my mic closer to her mouth.

"Ci-CAAAH-da," she said. I let it go. "Cicada three by Scott …" She stumbled over the poet's last name, looked at me for guidance, which I did not give, then moved into the poem's first lines.

"I am drawn to the empty husk / of the Cicada," she read as a truck rumbled past and people walked by, some staring. She kept going. Occasionally she mispronounced words, misread lines, corrected herself.

Earlier that morning, I had recorded other people at the fair reading the same poem. There was a man with a gravelly smoker's voice who said the last time he read poetry was in high school; a friend's aunt who was high-pitched and quick with nerves; a bushy, bearded fellow in overalls who beamed when I asked him to read, and then read as if every syllable was a proclamation:

"I. tug. care. full. y. at. this. kneel. ing. shell."

The knitter's voice was clear. She read the first stanza. Then the second, the third, the fourth. I lowered my head, listening intently as the poem she read relayed an encounter with the shell of a molted bug to a moment with a dying grandfather.

Midway through the fifth stanza, "When he breathes his body crackles / like," her voice broke. I looked up to see her wiping a tear from her cheek.

"Sorry," she managed to squeak out. I almost spoke. Instead, I held my breath. In that moment of silence, she explained that seven years earlier, her grandfather had died a painful death. Her family never talked about his final, ugly year.

"I think in a way we just don't want to remember him like that, but—but that was a big part of our memories of him, too."

Taking a tissue from her purse, she dabbed her running nose and finished reading.

"Looking at this almost empty shell, / wanting to crawl inside, / slip his skin over mine and emerge shimmering new, / to sing with my grandfather through one more dusk."

I said thank you and she exhaled.

"Cicada III" became the first Poetry to the People podcast. After recording several people reading and responding to the poem, I took the tape back to my office, uploaded it to my computer and turned the individual readings into a collaborative one: I layered voices on top of each other, left in the fumbles and added music. I kept in the woman's story about her grandfather's death. The man with the gravely smoker's voice, reflected on his own--he said he doesn't expect to live too long past sixty.

   Recording people on the street connects them to poetry. I've walked poem in hand, mic turned on, looking for people everywhere: state fairs, New York City, city parks, bars, diners and farmer's markets. I've approached self-conscious teenagers, old men with cigars, best friends, toothless folks. Taking poetry to the people doesn't work every time. Some hesitate. Some are unsure of their voices. Some protest the poem. Others outright refuse to be recorded. But every so often, I find a person--a carnival worker, a minister, a granddaughter--who stops in her tracks, reads the words on the page, and finds her own voice in the poem.

ABBY WENDLE
TULSA, OKLAHOMA
2013

"It really matters that great poems get written," said Ezra Pound — sounding a bit like Woody Guthrie — "and it doesn't matter a damn who writes them." Something to keep in mind, perhaps, when one initially picks up or thumbs through a poetry anthology of any sort, of any stripe, from any given part of this country (or planet). It also, of course, "really matters" that such poems get recited, get heard, get shared. That's the case being made by this collection of poems, I think, and I'm pleased to have been a part of its creation.

Some of the poems in this book were originally chosen and edited by myself for publication in the pages of This Land. They were thereafter digitally recorded and posted online by Abby Wendle for her ongoing Poetry To The People project. It's been great (and gratifying) to see (and hear) these poems leap from the page, as it were, and out into the wider world via Abby's endeavors. I thank her for that work, and I applaud it.

Thanks as well to all who have read or will read (and all who have heard or will hear) these poems. "From California to the New York Island," et al.

SCOTT GREGORY
POETRY EDTIOR
THIS LAND

and I got here
and began eating

Coming Home
Ken Hada

On Interstate 35 north
of Guthrie, driving through
evening shadows I pass
a rusting, stale green Chevy
bouncing along on bald tires
with a great antlered deer
tied across the tattered roof.

I see a good Oklahoma boy
driving grateful, his eyes locked
straight ahead toward home
where his bride and kids await
his arrival with meat for winter,
stories to tell, hope for better
days ahead strapped tight
to the wildness in our souls.

the number of heaven and earth
John Colburn

They stole chickens and
slaughtered cows
they castrated pigs
they cut the tails off piglets
they followed deer through the woods
shot them in their necks
they put out traps
they raised lambs then slit their throats
they hung animals upside down in their barns
the blood drained out
their guts were baskets
they carried babies or carried bread
downriver to grandmother's gut
in the fall they slaughtered and they boiled meat
they canned the meat and stored it
in root cellars in shelved rows
and other parts even brains
they used for sausage
and they tied horses to iron equipment
and whipped them
but the dogs just ran free
they put meat in a clearing
and waited for a bear
all of this meat is how I am

    my great grandfather stole three chickens

>   he was put in jail
>   he got out he had a stroke
>   then he could only swear
>   only from half his face
>   his wife lost her mind was
>   'committed' but when he died
>   she 'came out of it'
>   lived for years
>   never stole chickens

they caught fish and slid steel knives
into their bellies
they dreamt of animals
the animal terror went into their bodies
and they too lost their minds
coyotes came to speak to them
they killed other people
as they were told to
they kidnapped a Lakota woman
it was winter there was so much snow
and nothing to kill
they survived on potatoes and
canned meat and canned pears
so that I was born

>   and one day a rabbit bit the tip off my finger
>   and chewed it up
>   so we killed the rabbit

some of them lived with mules in Kentucky
or horses in Massachusetts
some of them turned their front yards

into pig wallows in Iowa
and they kept slaughtering
they bought guns and sows
and killed who they were told to kill
and made whiskey
and killed rabbits and raccoon and foxes
they poached and ran
or later drove their cars into ditches
and more of them went to jail
they wanted sex and families
they wanted to slaughter more animals
even a horse in the worst of times
they were ready
in their root cellars
and they sang about food and animals
they played guitars by the stove
or on porches
and more animals died and became songs
meat dripping everywhere
and I got here and began eating

    this morning I saw a rabbit in the driveway
    I saw its beautiful eye
    it was feminine
    it carried a baby it carried bread
    its eye was a womb
    I was given a heart-shaped basket
    made from dried plants
    and I rode it down the river
    I thought who is riding in the basket
    it feels like no one
    the incinerator came on at dusk

    in the old yellow sky
    and wolf-children came out
    their hair gone poisonous
    the people grew tired of raising them
    and rubbing pollen on their bodies
    grew tired of how years
    run together after dark

they kept their bodies warm to stay alive
they cut down trees
and burned them to boil water
they shaved the sheep
they spun and wove the wool
children watched the looms fill
they had to keep warm
and some of them burned animal shit
some burned oil from the ground
or oil from giant whales
hauled onto boats and hacked to pieces
and the chimneys glowed hot
the lanterns glowed
children slept near whatever could burn
the adults killed to stay warm
they killed to eat
they burned lost people passing through
and the children watched their faces melt

    he might be dying
    might have died several times already
    he has a face problem
    the face is no good and must be hidden
    there's the seed of a face in there

    all withered
    someone check his teeth
    looks like a thief
    like if you took a pine cone
    got it wet
    through magic it grew bigger
    and walked around
    he is the kind of person
    to squish in a machine
    press the juice out of
    or rip apart with horses
    pour boiling water onto
    shoot metal into
    tell him to keep moving
    or we'll set him afire

they wanted to stay warm
they wanted to make more children
the rivers flooded
they were alive but winter came on
night came too and they wrote letters
someone lit a candle
the church bell froze
a crow perched on the chimney meant
someone would die
a white dog on the road at night
was a spirit
a woodpecker at the window
meant prosperity
a coyote in the yard
meant bad luck and a hard winter
souls inhabited the fires

ancestors spoke from the mouths of fish
the cemetery glowed at night
an elk wandered up to the house
to deliver its message
how fire keeps the busy souls away
sunlight in the pines
wild turkeys half-mad along the road
long lines of eggs and mothers and
sunlight in their feathers
each evidence of glowing sound
mind expansion practice dream
the squirrel alive and
the hawk in its piece of sky
and they prayed for sanctuary
they dreamt of the number twelve
and of twelve gears
turning this world
through the levels of urge
and in their dreams
where celestial fruits fell
into twelve tributaries
they prayed to be absorbed
by the divine
but instead they woke up
and drank whiskey
and wanted to fight
they distilled moonshine
in Kentucky
they took amphetamines and kept working
kept killing
the word was sacred
so they didn't speak

they built El Dorado industrial parks
on the graves of each other
they built flashbulbs and stark faces
they built orchards and winding roads
and shudders for the windows
of homes they built or stole
and they built a word for us
they called us the future
and they kept killing
they got to twelve and they started over
the future was both heaven and earth
the gods the months the stars
a spiral of twelve
a fulfillment
an eating sound.

Ode to the Midwest
Kevin Young

*The country I come from
Is called the Midwest*
                —Bob Dylan

I want to be doused
in cheese

& fried. I want
to wander

the aisles, my heart's
supermarket stocked high

as cholesterol. I want to die
wearing a sweatsuit—

I want to live
forever in a Christmas sweater,

a teddy bear nursing
off the front. I want to write

a check in the express lane.
I want to scrape

Ode to the Midwest

my driveway clean

myself, early, before
anyone's awake—

that'll put em to shame—
I want to see what the sun

sees before it tells
the snow to go. I want to be

the only black person I know.

I want to throw
out my back & not

complain about it.
I wanta drive

two blocks. Why walk—

I want love, n stuff—

I want to cut
my sutures myself.

I want to jog
down to the river

& make it my bed—

I want to walk
its muddy banks

& make me a withdrawal.

I tried jumping in,
found it frozen—

I'll go home, I guess,
to my rooms where the moon

changes & shines
like television.

This poem originally appeared in the July/August 2007 issue of *Poetry* magazine

OG'S AND LEMONADE
Keiyetta Guyon

These new cool gangstas aint got nothing on the O.G.'s,
The original G.'s,
The Pistol packin, dynamite in petite packages, the 'child I'm
    old school I don't play dat,'
O.G.'s.
They demand that granddaughters wear the fluffiest dresses &
    the world's itchiest stockings
Shiny new shoes, pressed hair, curls too
Especially on Sundays when all the O.G.'s sit on the first &
    second pews quotin' all the scriptures & screamin
        "Amen Bishop, that's the truth!"
They rock the freshest curls from their ancient roller sets
Eyeglasses, O.G's don't mix contacts with cataracts
Red lipstick & snapping dentures, extra denture cream in the
    fanny pack
Up to neck shirts
Tucked into waistbands of pants & skirts
Knee high stockings & sneakers or other shoes that can never
    be worn to church
& on Sundays the fanny pack is replaced with the historic purse
The one that holds the candy store, the world's biggest belt &
    the pistol just in case somebody needs to get hurt
O.G.'s don't hustle but their bank accounts overflow
They get money from their first job & let that interest grow
Always buying what they want 'cuz they got money to blow
Thankful for life to live so they gotta live it up

Wake up
In the morning time just to see the sun come up
Rub the handle of Bessie the double barrel shot gun; come to
        rob the house you will get shot up
Slavin over hot stoves, skillets poppin C-R-I-S-C-O
Inhale the taste of bacon, exhale the taste of toast
Brew the fresh coffee, aroma make you wiggle yo toes
Spoiling
Spoiling is their field of work
Grandchildren's faces covered with sweets & never ending smiles
Puppies, chubby with wagging tales & smiling eyes
Hypocritical to spankings because discipline can only be given
        at certain times
& the look only burns holes when it comes from their eyes
Always resting in peace
Leaving those they loved to fight over what they loved &
Cherish memories sweeter than tropical punch kool-aid
This is a shoutout to every grandma, every true O.G. in America today
You are the sugar of life
How else could lemonade be so sweet?

Maybe Shawnee
Claire Edwards

On gravel roads
where you search for the heart of the American
Inn side sheets,
or between sheets,
an impossibility,
the possibility of
"oh!" and "oh, no"
of "right there"
and "slow your roll"
and "we'll get out of here
any
minute
now."

I swear.

The impossibility pressing up against
thighs and mouths
and the clumsy, tender
Now.

It'll be fun, now.
So don't be mad.

It's the impossibility of intellectual unequals
Rolling between-

    -we'll get up any minute now,
        I swear-
-between the audacity of sandwiches
        and skylines
        and-
I need a better metaphor
        Like I need a hole in the head
        Like I need a used condom
        Like I need a simile
Like I need
And I need
        To warm you up, ok?
Because this room is in Siberia,
        I swear.

        -we should be going,
            any second now.
But listen:

It's the possibility
In a fallen bra strap
        And ripe new shoulders
It's the hunger
        of hands
It's the innocence
        of bumper cars
And the promise
of a stairwell and a gravel road.

The Middle of Nowhere
Todd Boss

is always also
the center of some great somewhere. Once, at dinner

on a train through
Montana, I met a Loretta from Rugby, North Dakota—

the geographical center,
she said, of North America. Across from us was Peter

whose time in the military
meant he'd lived on six continents. When he spoke,

he was all soft consonants:
He was headed for Milwaukee where a leading dental

surgeon would continue
the year-long reconstruction of his teeth—currently

MIA—the casualty,
he said, by hundreds of hairline fractures, of 35 years

of war zone trauma.
Six continents, I repeated. And the silence that followed

facilitated a collective
reflection on the headlines of the past quarter century.

All the front   lines.
She from Rugby said only, "I just stay in Rugby, I

never go   anywhere,"
and when she said that, I felt a Midwestern tuning fork
go   bing!
in my bones. She shook her head. She said she never

went anywhere,   and yet
here she was and here we were together, in the dining car,

the presidential   mountains
sliding off the glass like melting snow on either side.

Suddenly I was   reminded
of the last sentence I'd read, in the observation car, from

a Denis Johnson   short story:
"The road we were lost on cut straight through the middle

of the   world."
Ladies and Gentlemen, this is your engineer speaking.

For the rest of   this afternoon
and well into this evening, we will be cutting straight

through the   middle
of the world. Please be sure to take it all in, both halves, on

both sides   of the train.
When you depart at your destination, you'll still be cutting

straight   through
the middle of the world, no matter which direction you go.

Please   remember
your belongings. Thank you. And should I tell you now

that we had   nothing
to say to one another over our desserts, Peter staring one way

out the window,   Loretta
the other, as if half the world were war, the other nowhere,

and never   the twain,
like parallel rails, criss-crossing? Well, no. Our talk in fact

was nonstop.   We
didn't have a moment to mark the world's bifurcated passing.

The Minneapolis Poem
Dobby Gibson

When I see an airplane pass overhead
I sometimes imagine there are celebrated poets
reclining inside the pressurized cabin,
flying over me on their way back and forth
between New York and San Francisco
to give thrilling readings to one another
and afterward sip chablis and laugh
knowingly about books I've neither heard of nor read.
When they look down briefly at the Mississippi River
I imagine they think of miserable James Wright
or miserable John Berryman,
or the strangely underwhelming poetry of Robert Bly.
Do they know the Microsoft of this little city
used to be that river, which powered the flour mills
that for some created great fortunes?
When I was young, one of the great mills exploded
after a squatter ashed his cigarette,
and a transformative civic fire raged into a cold night.
When it was over we drove past the ruins
the fireman had encased in beautiful sculptures of ice.
We sometimes still call this town Mill City
even though the last of the mill buildings
have been converted into multi-million dollar lofts
for retired financial services professionals,
with stainless steel restaurant-grade appliances,
and bathroom floors constructed of invisible tubes

carrying hot water to keep their feet warm when they step
    from the tub.
This is how it can feel looking down at the river
or last night up at the fragments of a space station shattering
as it reached the atmosphere through binoculars
manufactured by people in China
who are not allowed to read such news on the internet.
James Wright said Minneapolis is a horrible city
to commit suicide in because its waters are so often frozen.
I wonder whether he thought of those words
when he learned that John Berryman
had leapt from the Washington Avenue Bridge
onto the frozen ground of Bohemian Flats.
Later today my job, which is not the making of this poetry,
or the milling of flour, or the recovery of cosmic fragments
from the sea, will take me to the airport where strangers
will search my body and find nothing except this poem,
perhaps forgotten in my back pocket,
and after I tie my shoes I will share the concourse silently
with people who are passing through to other places,
and for as long as the moving sidewalk
pushes us past the cold windows
I'll delete tiny messages from my phone,
moving more quickly standing still than was once thought
    possible,
just enough clothes in my bag to get me home.

Driveway
Ron Padgett

Again I slid up over the horizon
and the lights of Tulsa spread flat out before me.
"Ah, there you are," I said,
"like a porch light left on
for almost thirty years."

"Don't get carried away,
Ron. Yes, the lights are on for you and anyone
else who wants to rush toward me in a stream of light,"
the awakened city said, "but I knew
it was you. Who else would talk to me like this?"
I said, "There always was this special thing between us,
no?"

"Between you and me,
not between me and you. You're like all the rest,
you think you're the only one to come along, that
I was made for you."

"I know, Tulsa, but
remember, I was an only child."

"I know, Ron, but
you're not a child now, so why act like one?
Why don't you settle back and take a deep, long look
at things the way they are? Why not just let go

of your love-hate thing with me? Do you really need
this longing and regret and so much useless anger?"

"But what'll I have of the me who was a little boy?"
"Whatever you already have, no more, no less,"
the voice said evenly.
Suddenly I cried
into the dark, "Where's your mouth?"
"You don't know? It's all around you"
I was pulling
into the driveway where I used to live
"it's your skin"
and opened my eyes and was
here, in New York, typing these lines.

Kaboom Pantoum
Kathy Fagan

I'll ring the bells,
Ohio, tomorrow,
when stars come due
like lice to a grackle.

Ohio, tomorrow
is winter, & every winter,
like lice on a grackle,
we must drive defensively.

This winter & every winter,
I wait too long to wear a coat.
We must dress defensively,
but last minute still counts.

If I wait to wear a coat,
will you wait with me?
Last minutes still count,
maybe more than last words.

Will you wait with me?
Take *sequoia*, for example—
maybe more than last words
word games reveal a lot—

sequoia, for example, is
the shortest word to use each vowel once.

Word games reveal a lot.
Short word. Tall tree. AEIOU.

The shortest word to use each vowel once
does not thrive in Ohio.
Short word. I double O. No UAE.
Bell in the mouth at either end.

Across the hot shore we walked toward our red hot baby

A Yarn for the Natural State
Steve Healey

I placed a jar in Tennessee
—Wallace Stevens,
"Anecdote of the Jar"

A jar placed us in Arkansas,
on a small island on a big lake.
A jar like God told us a yarn
about placing us there in Arkansas.
The yarn went round and round
that jar, and this is what it said:
to the lake we drove a pickup truck
past a billboard that said, "warning—
prepare to meet your God."
Then to the island on that lake
we drove a party barge preparing
to meet our God. We felt the hot sun
of Arkansas, we saw it turning
our skin red. So we drank cold beer
and sang songs about cold beer,
but still our skin turned red.
All around the wilderness sprawled,
round and round like a yarn
about trees. In that wilderness
we saw many antlered deer,
and those antlers repeated the shapes
of those trees. We saw inside
that wilderness like an ultrasound
repeating branchy antlers all around.

And as we saw, we began to believe
that we were in Arkansas to see
ourselves seen by that wilderness
that wanted like a chigger to bore
inside us and eat our skin cells.
Like the parasitic larvae of mites,
Arkansas wanted our bodies
to host a party, it wanted to eat us
like the baby we once made
inside us. And when our party barge
arrived at that small hot island,
there was our baby, standing on
the shore of shattered shale,
like an Arkansas chigger
wanting to bore inside us.
That jar-shaped island with its rim
of shattered shale, all around
the water wanting to pour inside it,
and our baby there, throwing
shale into the water. We'd forgotten
how to give birth to this baby,
and as we stepped onto that shore,
we felt the party barge giving
birth to us. On our red skin
we felt the hot sun of Arkansas.
Across the hot shore we walked
toward our red hot baby.
We saw him seeing us as a jar
that had placed him in Arkansas.
And when we asked, "Have you
seen our God?" he said to us,
"Have you seen our God?"

The 500
Richard Stull

We were too preoccupied with sex to know that our mothers were suffering so we jumped into a car one night and headed out for Indianapolis and the 500, a case of beer in the trunk. A few packs of Marlboros. Sometime before dawn in the parking lot of the Brickyard, a star fell into my lap. I stroked her flame and offered her a sip, I believe it was Idiot's Brew. It fell heavily upon us, and so we dreamed a page of the past. I asked her of her mother's suffering and was astonished that she knew nothing of it. We were on a slippery slope, a nuance from minute to minute. I invited her for a walk. The lot with its cars and drunks was a vast garden to us. Ornamental trees sprang from the foothills. Paths led to springs and their somber delights. Suddenly a shadow stepped from behind a tree. It was A. J. Foyt. "Kids, I've snatched glory from the talons of death and have laid it, a lost impatient image of love, at the pearls of your feet." A wind carried us instantly back to the car and my obscure friends, whom I have met once or twice since then but only in dreams. In one, we ford a creek just in time to find our homes and the town of our birth collapsed. In another, the gates to the garden are tarnished, and my star flees back to her heavy home. I remember the outer surface of the race, but the speed of time has transformed everything.

When I was a kid...
Doug Claybourne

I tortured horny toads
when I was a kid
I don't feel good about that
but I did –
I surrounded em
with lighter fluid mostly
shot match sticks into the sky
lit fires in my eyes.
I remember thinking
jeez - it's just a horny toad,
but I was wrong
and I should have known better.
Frogs, ants, grasshoppers
I've exploited my share or better
run over em - and
burned some out of their dirt homes.
I was trouble I admit it
when I was a kid I
lit those fires around em
mostly with hand made match guns
shooting' high over Joe Creek
as I just didn't have a sense
of anyone getting hurt
me - or anyone else
for that matter
not mean spirited of course

I was just a dumb kid
seen now as a grown up
and looking back and forth.
I never hurt a dog
but I threw some cats against walls
as we heard they always landed standing up
and I told ya before
I'm not proud of it,
but I don't think I did
any real harm to cats
they all meowed after
and came back for the milk
and food that my
little sister always fed em.
And we didn't throw em that hard
it's not like they bounced or anything
or yelped or screamed
but they did land on all fours
just like they said.
In junior college,
I had a German Sheppard
that ate the hamburger meat
I left up on a counter—ten pounds of it
purchased for a party
lucky he didn't eat my roommates marijuana as
that stuff was in 10 gallon trash bags.
I wasn't playing with frogs
or horny toads anymore
I was listening to
"Hot August Night" and The Doobie Brothers
and wondering if I would ever
get out of Tulsa.

When I was a kid...

I did finally
But then of course
you never really get out of your home town
it's always in your blood
we learn as we get older
it's a part of your DNA
it's like the air you breathe.

When I was a kid
I used to like to go down
to Joe Creek and throw skip-rocks
across the water
look for crayfish and tadpoles
it was pretty simple back then
call a buddy
find a stick and take a pocketknife,
and just hang out on a Saturday
that's it – but it's not so simple these days I guess.

Karma, Oklahoma
Caleb Puckett

As I puzzled over the position of Karma, a bony waitress at a roadside café swept up all my change and explained how the Red River had washed the place away long ago, leaving a ghost town whose only crop now consists of farm folk germinating underground until midnight arrives and they burst beyond the Texas border in search of those dry counties where they can count on a truly Western sense of law and order.

Hard Luck Okie
Roy Turner

In that dear state of Oklahoma
in the city where buildings are high
I laid on my pillow so hopeless
looking through my tin shack at the sky.

I got up early next morning
out in the cold I did creep
walked off without any breakfast
and left two hungry babies asleep

And then I left that big city,
I walked down 60 highway
I had a good reason for leaving
so I headed for Pacific Bay

Then I seen the Texas cotton
and the Mexico bottomless lakes
and the Arizona healy monster
and the big diamond rattlesnakes

One night I heard the little coyotes,
I listened to their pitiful whine
I wondered if the poor little creatures
didn't have hungry babies like mine

That same night I dreamed of my father

he said boy don't never go back
he said give them diamonds your part of that city
and that little old rusted tin shack

I started this poem in the desert
my bed lying out on the ground
then covered up my hungry babies
and smoked a cigarette and laid down.

Then I picked peas in California
from two to six hampers a day
trying to make a few pennies
to drive that old hungry away

Oklahoma farewell.

This poem was recorded by the Library of Congress at a migrant farmer's camp in California in the late 1930s.

The Stringtown Prison Blues
Stringtown Prison Poetry Workshop

This time is so hard to do here, I think I'll go and pray.
I say this time is so hard to do here, I think I'll just go and pray.
But someone just tol me gawd went on a holiday.

In Stringtown Prison the men number four-one-eight.
Yeah, I say in Stringtown Prison the men number four hundred, one-eight.
Cross this lonely country, 418 women wait.

Oh I'm so lonely Lord, I wish somebody would write.
I say I'm so lonely Lord, I wish somebody would just write.
Let the dog bark in the envelope and even that'll be all right.

Well you and I are the only ones left baby, the only ones left alive.
Yeah baby, I say you and I are the only two goddamn people left alive.
And now here you are telling me that I should take a dive.

This place is a cemetery, folks, each cell a cold tombstone.
I say this place is a cemetery, people, and each cell is a cold tombstone.
The spirit of decay just seeps deep into your bone.

My baby says she wrote me, and I know what she says is true.
Yeah, my baby says she wrote me, and I know what she says is true.
But somebody robbed the stagecoach carrying the mail and

now what'm I gonna do?

Lord it was better when I had some wine to drink.
Yes Lord, it was a helluva lot better when I had some cheap
 wine to drink.
But now I ain't got wine but only time to sit and think.

Yes Lord, I'm out of marijuana, out of uppers too.
I say I'm clean outta marijuana, and out of uppers too.
The guards are on a rampage, and boy am I sure blue.

Gonna leave this joint one day folks, and I ain't lookin' back.
Say I'm gonna leave this joint one day folks and ain't ever
 lookin' back.
Gonna catch the next thing rollin' and hope it don't jump the track.

From Warning Hitch Hikers May Be Escaping Convicts, 1980, Moonlight Publications.

I tend a stinging nettle patch

Back Roads
Laura Brandenburg

The explosions are always real.
Small wheels turn tighter.
These stark prairie towns
    keep the eyes and bones close to the grind.

Any eight-year-old knows
    the back roads to the next county,
    knows that things must bleed, that flies
    frantic in an empty house
    always mean something.

A girl with leftover bruises
    sits on the dark steps, a gun in her lap.
The dog cocks one sad-eyed brow
    and rests his anvil head at her feet.
Her pant legs are wet from long grass,
    from dew and sweat, from every step
    that whispered, "Someplace...someplace...someplace."

Some work is serious in a small town.
Nobody falls down, nobody calls the cops.

EMPTY NEXT SYNDROME
Paula Cisewski

I don't consider myself
an overly dramatic person,
so it can be uncomfortable

to live on this ambulance planet.
Yet it's getting easier to be alone, even
when I'm not pleased with myself.

Isn't it amazing we each seem separate from anybody?
By contrast, isn't it mundane how in some contexts,
we are all reduced to lists of symptoms?

I tend a stinging nettle patch.
In sunlight, I can feel like a swept church.
This muted feeling, though.

Even if I could, I don't know what
I would invoke. Hey, rabbits
in the abandoned lot, what is

the exact opposite of a snake? If now it's darkening,
is rain coming, or night? In the distance, a siren
whines. Like clockwork. I can't save anyone.

Sowing Ohio
Rochelle Hurt

Housebound in this town, love yellows.
        Stay, and watch the walls peel away
from their ceilings.
                Look through this window:
    a mother stretches herself, and pulls
at the roof, little blanket feigning escape.

Her skin is sallow and singed
like a letter rescued from a fire.
                      Behind her
in their Sunday dresses, two daughters bend,
        hinged at the middle, and spend
                hours scouring the curry-colored rug—
something lost, a button popped.

Their dark hair's turned tawny,
        the color of searching too long,
        color of color gone.

A miniature twister turns itself dizzy
        and blows figure-eights through the room.

Husks, the daughters ripple
        and tip, then pick themselves up again.
The walls flutter as the long-armed mother
holds them.

Sowing Ohio

        Upstairs, a father is whispering,
    I want to live, forever
           climbing out the window.

See how easily it all comes down—
how quickly the table kicks off its legs;
    how the light bulbs drop
        into the yellow sea of carpeting;
how the blinds break apart
           and scatter like leaves;
how the house only wants to shake
    itself down to a fistful of seeds
        cast wide across its square lot of wheat.

Spare Me Yellow Skies
Wilma Elizabeth McDaniel

Temperature is 105
high pressure puts
a hateful cap on our
heads
and holds it there

Under a sullen mustard
sky
that will not relent
and weep us rain

My poor house suffers
as much as I
the tiny patio
would gladly move to Pismo Beach

The cactus in Mama's pottery
jar
has turned to gray mush
and the neighbor
with all the terrible secrets
has not opened her drapes
today

I pull my drapes wide open
and ask myself again
why does a yellow sky
trouble me
I have loved blue skies
and purple
madly
gray and black
I have embraced as sisters

but someone spare me yellow
skies

Sorry. Sorry. Sorry.
Hannah Brooks-Motl

Say you say you lived here once and I believed this

Thinking bars aren't homes, nor travel, when he kissed me I was denatured

We sit in the truck and are not bad

As little kids playing dirty in some snow

Their road the small part of a bigger

What we own is ours like weakness in the coffee or pride

Is everything I can explain away about myself like

What's killing is the weather color

No milk in the river

I apologize for my fatness

Sorry. Sorry. Sorry.

its midnight insides are the size of the world

The Ease of Trout
Jeffrey Skemp

where the road descends
steeply as it twists
like gorgeous wreckage

and there is always brightness
like water
like gravel
like the clicking of ants
full of rain and covered in dust

like a child
have you ever dreamed you drowned
in the shallow creek at night?

its cold insistent ripples fill you
and there you witness
the ease and indifference of trout

their shiny black eyes
the quiet glass buttons you dug up
in the middle of the woods

sometimes midday in your backyard
the dying maple tree
vibrates full of sleeping cats

sometimes seconds before a storm
silence has an echo

and there is always brightness
like fire
like leaves
like the creaky old barn
at night
becomes the perfect cave

under a sky of infinite tin
its midnight insides
are the size of the world

and you are the only one
who can see in the dark

Falling and Rising
John Brehm

Was it then I knew or then I began
to forget, that day on the bank
of the Blue River when

my brother tried to get
me to see a bullfrog or a bird
perched somewhere and I leaned

out over the water seeing nothing
but sepia-toned Nebraska, weeds
and cottonwoods and clouds

billowing like buffalo overhead,
there, there, he said, until I
reached the body's limit

of standing slanted straining and
fell into swiftly moving river
headfirst under the cold

and dark and saw dark
quick shapes rising dancing
before then into and beyond my eyes,

witches, I said later, they looked
like witches, and wanted me,

those black and wavering circles-

was that what I was meant
to see, world beneath the world,
before my father caught me

by the ankle and hauled me up,
sputtering little nearly taken traveler?
Is that the pulse I look for

still, the sense of something darkly
flowing just below the surface
making everything

here feel wrong? What were
those shapes, where were they going?

From *Sea of Faith*, 2004, University of Wisconsin Press.

FOX FACE, SNOW FACE
Sun Yung Shin

"I needed to turn this cemetery
inside out"

김혜순
Kim Hyesoon

Which body, black marker, black acre, dark and darker

Eat brick, baseball bat baby, rat baby, shed rabbit

Sun snow, a thousand skins, stack and flag

Stitched along the seams, a game of moveable figures

Eyes, wild, a face without a door

Am I alive

So much depends on

Do I not grow like a child, cloud, cloth, camp, shadow, shutter—

Brought here, bought here, saved here

Under glass, new sky, lung and eye

Pierce his foot, shepherd then shepherd

A tent to kill and eat from the inside

A mother, father, dragon, tether

Blood and wine and ribs and wheat

Who, am, I, to, ruin, this, fatal, plain

Recurrence
Michael White

your voice at a Utah phone booth
trying to tell me what they'd found

sunrise on West Texas salt flats
silence difficult to bear

I was nodding off as I-10 bent
dissolved beneath the lick of heat

that blistered paint on my truck's hot hood
so I punched myself as hard as I could

each fist into the opposite thigh
till I couldn't hold the pedal down

the Guadalupe Mountains floating
past my shoulder midday but

I wasn't really there myself
I was immolated wreathed in flame

as flurries of tremors swept my frame
when a thunderhead ahead caught fire

there was no way out but through

Untitled
Jim Moore

The gray morning and the rain, the wind and the bridge. The Falls falling so furiously. Our friend in her last days; wheelchair only; find me some fucking quince! Then smiling, delighted to still be desperate for pleasure. Quince jam laced with cannabis. But her low goofy laugh is gone now, the one that denoted wind and soft rain, a dawn that would never die inside her. All that gone. Now her husband watches every move, pushing her chair past the Falls falling. So furiously. So furious. Slouch hat low enough to cover his eyes from now until the end.

He keeps the way he's been touched
in the pockets of his jacket

Ticket to Ride
Melody Charles

the problem is that you want the storm
to gather, to come together to get
her a ticket to ride the waves
of moments upon moments upon
moments later, opening the door,
she breathes out and out and
out of the closet overstuffed with
close that old door and open your
many new windows rolled down in
the rain, what relief, the flash and
rumble with yourself, the struggle
to trust in a dormant strength
of the winds exceeding one
hundred miles to the next rest
stop running that narrative: be still

Rapture
Miss Terri Ford

We are the plastic children, flying toward the sun.
We are the infirm rising through rooftops, we are the real
housewives of Duluth, our dresses blown above
our cheeks, we are the dads jetting above the jigsaws,
weedwackers. And the dead in their nightclothes or
La-Z-Boys or under the sea: all of us steering
with superheroic outstretched arms, into blue, beyond –

Except for those of us with our faces to the sky and our shoes
still here. We are astonished, some of us weeping, in
fear or because of beauty in spectacle, with the blind ones at
our sleeves asking what, the wind, and why. Recover
to tell them: We are not plastic children. We are
not flying. We are here, at home on the earth.

Autobiography
Joe Brainard

---I was born in Tulsa, Oklahoma in 1942.
---No, I wasn't. I was born in Salem, Arkansas in 1942. I always say I was born in Tulsa tho. Because we moved there when I was only a few months old. So that's where I grew up. In Tulsa, Oklahoma.
---A lot has happened between then and now, but somehow, today, I just don't feel like writing about it. It doesn't seem all that interesting. And it's just too complicated.
---What's important is that I'm a painter and a writer. Queer. Insecure about my looks. And I need to please people too much. I work very hard. I'd give my right arm to be madly in love. (Well, my left.) And I'm optimistic about tomorrow. (Optimistic about myself, not about the world.) I'm crazy about people. Not very intelligent. But smart. I want too much. What I want most is to open up. I keep trying.

Nude in the City
Regina DiPerna

Your hands on newspapers, your hands
in your hair. Is your body yours to undress?

Or is someone across town sketching you
into unimaginable positions? An ex lover? The stranger

you brushed past on the sidewalk?
So often you'd like the world to be plotted on a straight line

of storefronts, glass windows hiding diners,
men leaning out of wine bars. But the world is a crush of color.

See scarlet. Copper. The color of lips, lungs. See
nude. See a man buying a cup of coffee

in an American city.
Now look at his neck, the shades

of flesh —nude, apricot— flourishing between nape
and Adam's apple. It's autumn and that's all you can see

of his body, except hands unjamming from pockets to reveal
a quarter or some dimes, first in his fingers, then in his

open palm. You can't see the muscles of his thighs
tighten, can't know the shape of sternum

hidden beneath layers of shirt.
He keeps the ways he's been touched

in the pockets of his jacket. You want to see him
slip it down, see his shoulders bared,
see him discard sleeves of leather, silhouettes.
But you can only see

a blur of light and rust. The city. The crush
of slate and smoke stacks he recedes into,

hands veiled in his pockets, then
hands exposed in the cold air.

The Orange Grove Is Beautiful This Time Of Year:
Nick Weaver

I know a girl who calls herself a witch.
When she was little she sang sing songs and watched Sesame Street.
She races broomsticks down hallways and climbs staircases
    like an arctic explorer.

Her bed is pastel pink,
her window is always open so she can smell the orange grove outside,
the breeze makes her paper mâché butterflies shudder, and
    flutter, and swarm.

She loves singing for her mother, she loves riding her father's shoulders
she loves her brother's Hot Wheels track, and she loves the
    witching game
because that's when magic becomes real.

Lacing the bodices on last year's Halloween costume,
she lays Ken and Barbie on her bed spread,
brews a potion out of Play-Dough and bubble juice,
her tiny hands make plastic come alive,
the miniature lovers talk about reality TV like the grown-ups do.
The scent outside makes the witch giggle,
her wild hair shudders, and flutters, and swarms.
Her heart is a metronome that counts a beat each for the fingernails,

the eyelashes, the baby teeth,
everything she sheds to grow.

Because the day she got too big for shoulders was the day
 the orange grove rotted,
and she started wondering what she was doing wrong,
the spells she was casting couldn't bring back her haircuts,
her height markings on the door frame,
she had to amputate the scraps of her past she was just
 starting to salvage.

So she stopped playing with spellbooks
and tortured her feet into ballet slippers,
the witch learned to dance,
and her mother would grab her by the shoulders and turn her
 in perfect circles,
inspecting her bedazzled scrunchy for unmanageable tangles
as if she was feeling for tears in a package of her second-skin
 pantyhose.

And as the years ticked by,
as she learned magic didn't exist,
as all her grandparents died
and she learned to lay out funeral clothes,
as she stopped having a taste for citrus,
the metronome in her heart slowed down to an auditory ground zero.

She counts beats per minute in the men who use her like a food bank,
the women stuffing specter daughters into the pageantry they
 never found in themselves.
The people fragile like clay dolls, the plastic people she used
 to puppet with her mind.

The Orange Grove Is Beautiful This Time Of Year:

It used to scare me how much she loved her hair,
now it scares me how easily she can cut it off.

She's the girl who declaws hobbling high-heels,
the girl tired of being chained to a clearance sale front door.
She's the girl who stows old magic away in secret perfume bottles
and uses the fermented oils to make her skin blossom again.

I want to sketch a vista for her,
rewind the metronome, lay down newspaper in her heart
help her paint a mural of the forest that once lay outside her window.
I want to help her become the woman she longs to be.

I watch her walk a twisted blueprint path from drug store to
    drug store,
and all the pharmacies are full of new concoctions to save her,
there's a shortage in her drug supply, but there's no shortage
    of drugs in her life.

Because I'm worried about the things she's brewing now,
mixtures of Xanax and broken hearts and trashy lipstick,
she's trying so hard to leave the cauldron behind and just be normal.
I want to tell her how much I love the sorcery she breeds in her blood.

And I think about the things I want to tell my daughter,
the girl who will love Halloween, the girl with wild hair like mine,
unshackling her heart to explore the jungle in her bedroom,
she'll play the witching game,

And I'll tell her that magic is always real.
It doesn't stop existing when you stop believing in it.

I'll tell her how precious the orange grove was.
And how to make the sweetest juice from the ripest pulp.

I will tell my daughter how beautiful beauty is,
and how beautiful magic is,
and how beautiful you were,
and how beautiful she will be,
and how beautiful this time is,
while she still brews potions,
and calls herself a witch.

thrtthr whthrrthms
Maria Damon

Thursday, March 04, 2004

am i tran
sforming
thispace
?
friendly
takeover
?
o dare i
!
watch me
!

                10:04 AM

Wednesday, November 05, 2003

spendrifth nightmoth
mouthope nnnnnn
didn't meander
but so snaky like
lady ishmael is mmmmm
hirsty ttttt
make it now

                3:37 PM

Wednesday, September 17, 2003

ah neverbee
yr the one 4 me
come put your hand in my tree
n we can b 3.
oh lushable crumbcake
please crush the velvet
                              11:49 AM

Thursday, December 04, 2003

the oneliness of i
is all about a love
of lines and friends
of ness and of lees
those crags and bur-
rows you abide by i
and i by you.
                              1:07 PM

Monday, September 08, 2003

i love to read you up
side down back to the
beginning of word-
time all lush pillow-
yellow in finally down
now to hammock laze-
d
peace in rest ah
summer
                              8:55 AM

In The Field

Michael Madonick

The red fox flashes in the field, and the mind
wants to stop it. Run the catalogue of what
it knows, put a hen-house, chicken wire, a farmer
with his shotgun, dogs baying in their ribs
right behind it. It's flash cards, kindergarten,
the pull string toy that makes animal sounds.
What sound does a fox make? It's a comet's
tail in the high dark of the sky, running
the thin woods, gone in a whisker. Cat
on fire, who stole the eggs, the fence needs
crimping, it runs on its toes. It's the blood
the synapse lights, roman candles, electric
in the skull, sly as the moon ducking in clouds.
Friction likes a partner, side-kick to flame, the boa
of its tail, incorrigible as snake. The thing's
a long way gone before you know it, before
the fox is a fox flashing in the field. The mind
wants to stop it, run it over, press repeat, treat it
like the prom corsage, play it till it's done, the music
of its running, running like a fox, leap and jaunt,
leap and jaunt, more leap than run. Sometimes
the mind cannot hold what it sees, plays it in its sleep,
dreams it in the night, works it in its crib. The heart,
the heart, my friend, the fox is the heart, and the mind
cannot stop it, it's flashing in the field.

timing
Odalee Still

i squish my fiery stick
into black plastic
walk through a
long white echo and
find you
near the end
of a nearly empty table
filling up

i sit beside you
seconds before
a gay man comes
squeals with delight
at the beautiful boy
with beautiful hair
strolling in to his right

a flushed blue eyed flirt sits
talks about bees
a dark lady with waves
wiggles her hips
a big boy on her heels
giggles and giggles
and gives and gives

after the entree
you write me a love letter
in fingerprints on a fork

timing

you stick in my boot
i slide beneath your right thigh
you snatch up, slip inside my purse

-

the words you wrote
the day before said
you left once to New Orleans
in search of the crossroads
where Katrina and Voodoo meet

you met a warlock
the warlock told you
these things:
You have the knowledge of God.
You will find new work.
You will meet a quarter century old woman
who will change your life.
You will go out with a bang

bang
bang
here we sit
i am
twenty-five
1 + 5, 26
i am
forty-one
seventy-seven
       thirty-three
one-hundred-six
hyphenated
plussed
time

before i knew
i could exist

-

in the parking lot
streetlamp yellow casts
on my four door sedan
on your hands
on our boots straddling
the shadow of
outside
with the openness of in

we lean into the hot metal
melt through
and sit
in a hundred and a thousand degree heat
you ask me
what it is that

i want. need.
i blink. think.

long for us to sit so long
we turn to stone
ache for stone against stone
to rub so slow
it takes a millennium
to turn to sand
live in so much light
we become ivory
piano keys you play alone
in a home we share

life goin' on
goin' on
goin' on

Through a Country
Joel Stein

You, on the one hand, see a land
Green and rolling
With chalky marble
And stretches of yellowed sandstone
Patched here and there into the hills,
Coming up for air after eons of sleep.

While I on the other hand say
Here collisions occurred
A hundred million moons ago
With valleys heavy and damp
And sea islands becoming rock above the clouds.

But now all of this
Comes to bear upon
Exit 49, a place
Of rest,
Of a chosen view,
The geometric fields left half fallow, half
In hope of an early spring,
A pause on our way home.

The time continues
One stop past this moment.
Clairvoyant for a mortal hour
We finish what is in our cup
Then climb back into our debate
As to where the best place is

To eat, to die, or
Start anew.

The land moves down to the sea
And the sea relents
It is getting ready
To begin again.

Jazz on a Diamond-Needle Hi-Fi
Deborah J. Hunter

Mama dropped the needle and my heart jumped.
It was fascinating, titillating,
be-boppin', foot stompin', traffic stoppin', biscuit soppin',
donut dippin', daytrippin', corn sippin',
make me wanna shout,
cuss somebody out;
it was without a doubt,
the most sinfully rappin', toe-tappin',
thigh slappin', happenin' event.

It was the sun risin', moon smilin',
bees hummin', lovers comin',
mamas cryin', souls dyin',
life goin' on
goin' on
goin' on.

It was Coltrane shatterin' shackles,
Bird making the night air moan,
Dizzy gettin' busy with the brass,
Brubeck redefining time,
Miles moving mountains meter by meter,
Ella bouncing lightning bolts off the sky.

It was jazz.
Ooh, jazz.
Yeah, jazz.
It was ss-ss-ss-ss-ss-ss

jazz.

BULL WHIPPOORWILL
Merrill Gilfillan

Aprils in the schoolyards
 boys paired off--one small, one tall,
 the little riding the big lad's back--
 for the Chicken Fights:

bantam centaurs circling
and charging, trying to unseat
the counterpart jockey and win the hour.
A little girl cheers.

All this survives full summer,
the Peace of Utrecht, several world wars.

And Queen Anne's lace gets better by the year.

Cicada III
Scott Aycock

I am drawn to the empty husk
of the Cicada
where it clings to the bark of a tree
in my backyard.

Fearing I will crush it,
I tug carefully at this kneeling shell
praying for one more day
past its allotted thirty.

I carefully cup the empty form
in my two hands
to carry to where my grandfather knells
on his side in bed.

He clings to a blanket drawn tight under his chin.
He is an insect.
His frail husk of a body
light enough that I could lift him.

The thin skin of his forearms
stretches tight over bones that once cradled me.
When he breathes his body crackles
like wax paper in fire.

Looking at this almost empty shell,
wanting to crawl inside,
slip his skin over mine and emerge shimmering new,
to sing with my grandfather through one more dusk.

Cleaning Graves in Calvert
Quraysh Ali Lansana

For Papa Johnny Hodge, my great-great grandfather

under a crying elder willow
we meet the 107 degree shade
bearing thirsty earth
from which i sprang.

a safehouse next door to
a tinderbox church.
sanctuary from hot

lone star nights.
though your face is hidden
i feel you in the folds of mama's hands.

calling beyond the tired summer
crops to bring us here.

we were the last to know
ritual precedes emancipation.

Cardiology
Nicklaus Faith

One.
Heart melts into ink.
Burns in the Arctic eternal night.
Melts snow to drips.

One.
Drip drips down manicured lawns. Fills thirsty, floral bellies.
Absorbs light.

One.
Day I'll move this tower of stone.
And launch your brain into space.
Children of your children will sail past
Oh   so   slow.

One.
Child will spend his Weekends in a brothel in Spain.
The year of Our Lord one-thousand nine-hundred and thirty-three.
He will drink port and smoke French cigarettes.

One.
Cigarette will burn down a forest.
Give your legacy cancer.
Cause the heart to quicken her tempo.

Cardiology

Two hearts, glued together. . . .

Thunder growls through glistening teeth,
Exploring sonic sea-scapes. . . .
One low rumble.

Oh, One.
Bug dead on the moving sidewalk at O'Hare.
Brief images from the grandiose life it led. How vast.
One bug heart, and mine, and yours.

Ascension

Jack Wendle

"I loved that damned hill
Climbing up that god damned-hill."
Carve on my grave stone.

Ascension

Poets
on the Middle of America

How do you know you're in the middle of America?
What do you see, hear, feel, taste, touch, smell?
Who's there with you?
What do you do?

Scott Aycock – Cicada III

"Oklahoma, to me, is the heart of middle America and its red dirt roads are the arteries criss-crossing the landscape, connecting earth, sky, and water. To stand here is to stand at the crossroads of Route 66, the Trail of Tears, the Dust Bowl; a place you leave and a place you never leave, no matter where you come to rest your feet."

Scott Aycock was born in Marked Tree, Arkansas, and now lives in Tulsa, Oklahoma.

Todd Boss – The Middle of Nowhere

"The middle of America is a place where, when you turn to address a stranger, you're met with willingness, not suspicion. The middle of America still has a relationship with the sky. We may be fly-over country, but at least there's a sky to fly in. The middle of America smells like cowshit and corn tassel."

Todd Boss was born in Marshfield, Wisconsin, and currently lives in Saint Paul, Minnesota.

Joe Brainard – Autobiography

Joe Brainard was born in Salem, Arkansas, and his ashes were scattered in northern Vermont after his death in 1994.

Laura Brandenburg – Back Roads

"The blonde woman from 203 is in the shade-free parking lot, kicked back in a lawn chair on the bed of her silver pick-up truck. She snaps the elastic at the waist of her pink polka-dot bikini and smokes a cigarette: the ocean could be anywhere."

Laura Brandenburg was born in French Lake, Minnesota, and now lives Minneapolis, Minnesota.

John Brehm – Falling and Rising

"I have not lived in the Midwest for many years, but whenever I go back I feel the uniquely nourishing mixture of boredom and subtle beauty that made me want to become a poet—the sense that something magical is brewing just under the relentless and not-totally-convincing ordinariness of things."

John Brehm was born in Lincoln, Nebraska, and currently lives in Portland, Oregon.

Hannah Brooks-Motl – Sorry. Sorry. Sorry.

"When I go home I cannot get over the sky. I take pictures of it on my phone, and send those pictures to my friends where I live now. 'The sky, the Midwest,' is the invariable caption. It's so impressive, so grand—there is so much of it, a kind of surplus of horizontalness. And then the grandeur of the sky feels unsettled by the tiny pin pricks of silo, and everything is at once somehow in one's periphery—cow, barn, parking lot, roadside bar—but also right out in front, and center, right there."

Hannah Brooks-Motl was born in Milwaukee, Wisconsin, and currently lives in Easthampton, Massachusetts.

Melody Charles – Ticket to Ride

"Tulsan train whistles and gasoline and endless green—country that burns as well as the foothills, falls further behind, but points her to a wider view."

Melody Charles was born in Tulsa, Oklahoma, where she lives.

Paula Cisewski – EMPTY NEXT SYNDROME

"I live in Minneapolis, but perhaps because I was born in Bemidji, Minnesota, home to a famous Paul Bunyan and Babe tribute, I am intensely fond of the fiberglass or concrete statuary by which small Midwestern towns often identify."

Paula Cisewski was born in Bemidji, Minnesota, and now lives in Minneapolis, Minnesota.

Doug Claybourne – When I was a kid...

"Route 66 for me is about the 'middle of America,' now there is very little left of it, but it use   two lane highways, small towns and churches. Wi[two lane]   on Sunday morning, along that hig   rch 'til after noon and no matter wh   ia— it's extreme—hot or cold... and

Doug Claybourne was born in Houston, Texas, and now lives in Brooklyn, New York.

John Colburn – the number of heaven and earth

"My whole family digs into the earth, hoping to find a cloud. This must be the middle of America; I feel upside down."

John Colburn was born in Mantorville, Minnesota, and now lives in Minneapolis, Minnesota.

Maria Damon – thrtthr whthrrthms

"I know I'm in the Midwest because the sky is huge and unpopulated. Nothing moves and it's either hot, sticky, and blindingly bright or, in the winter, dry and lung-numbingly cold."

Maria Damon was born in New York City, and now lives in Minneapolis, Minnesota.

Claire Edwards – Maybe Shawnee

"We are greeted by controlled burns on either side of that impossible road that promises bison and a good, hard look at the earth from a time when it was new. So we drive into a wall of smoke that looks just the most like the absolute edge of the world, desperate and hungry for some symbol of rebirth, not knowing we are already balls deep in it."

Claire was born, raised, and lives in Tulsa.

Regina DiPerna – Nude in the City

"I knew I was in Middle America when the cornfield across the road from my childhood home was razed and replaced with a series of prefab houses."

Regina DiPerna was born in Medina, Ohio, and now lives in Wilmington, North Carolina.

Kathy Fagan – Kaboom Pantoum

"A sunset lasts where land is flattest.
Where can it hide?"

Kathy Fagan was born in New York City, and now lives in Worthington, Ohio.

Nicklaus Faith - Cardiology

"On a summer night:
Thoughts of youth in the dry grass,
June Bug orchestra."

Nicklaus Faith was born in Tulsa, Oklahoma, where he still lives.

Miss Terri Ford - Rapture

"Clearly you know you're in middle America b/c of the dang FOOD. My grandma is famous for making lime green jello with lima beans and a soup she called "borscht" which had every vegetable in the world in it except ... beets. Mid-America also tastes like Kraft macaroni & cheese, a slab of iceberg lettuce, Spanish rice in the pressure cooker.

There are four seasons in middle America, though Minnesota really seems to fake spring like a bad joke. If you can drive a car with a clutch up and down the icy hills of Duluth, Minnesota, where I was born, you can do anything. There's a moment when the car is sliding when I always feel fascinated, in mid-air in the middle of America -- where will I end up, where am I going?"

Miss Terri Ford c urrently lives in Minneapolis, Minnesota. In triumph.

Dobby Gibson – The Minneapolis Poem

"'The middle of America' isn't a place so much as it is an idea America defines itself against. So from wherever one stands, it's always somewhere farther down the road. It's like outer space: simultaneously everywhere and no-place at all."

Dobby Gibson was born in Minneapolis, Minnesota, where he lives.

Merrill Gilfillan – BULL WHIPPOORWILL

"I drive the smallest roads I can find as often as possible, in long shapeless loops—as both a celebration of continental space and a substitution for saltwater near at hand—and know I have reached the right place when meadowlarks outnumber people by at least 50 to 1."

Merrill Gilfillan was born in Mount Gilead, Ohio, and now lives in Denver, Colorado.

Keiyetta Guyon – OG'S AND LEMONADE

"The word 'y'all' is a part of everyday vocabulary. Chicken Fried Chicken is the best thing ever, and it's offered at many of the more formal restaurants. Cowboy boots are a fashion statement. When there is a storm warning for Oklahoma, people are outside looking at the sky, playing basketball, driving around, or sitting on their porches. Very few people take cover."

Keiyetta Guyon was born in Tulsa, Oklahoma, where she lives.

Ken Hada – Cross Timbers

"Sundown in the Crosstimbers: I look east and smell green pines and lavender Chicory in the Ouachita. I look west and see golden prairie grass and the rusty-peach feathers of Scissortails in flight."

Ken Hada is from Ada, Oklahoma, where he lives.

Steve Healey – A Yarn for the Natural State

"In the middle of America there's a lot of empty space, in the cities and fields and skies, in the Dairy Queens and Waffle Houses, in the way people think and feel and talk and relate to each other. Sometimes the empty space is ignorant and afraid and lonely; sometimes it's beautiful and liberating."

Steve Healey was born in Washington, D.C., and now lives in Minneapolis, Minnesota.

Deborah J. Hunter – Jazz On A Diamond-Needle Hi-Fi

"You know you're in Middle America when you overhear the following, 'I never had allergies until I moved here.' "

Deborah J. Hunter was born in Tulsa, Oklahoma, where she lives.

Rochelle Hurt – Sowing Ohio

"In the middle of America, there is no ocean to keep the time, so the past mingles with the future in odd ways: rust on the skyline, the smell of a closed paper mill in the middle of a corn field, dandelions pushing through the floor of an old factory. It's what I imagine being inside of a surrealist painting might be like—at once familiar and startling, desperate and resilient."

Rochelle Hurt was born in Youngstown, Ohio, and now lives in Chapel Hill, North Carolina.

Quraysh Ali Lansana – Cleaning Graves in Calvert

"playing hooky
for jimbo

sitting here with you watching
middle america gnaw on itself

newlyweds roll their newborn
past a silver speedboat

its sleek design, promise of adventure
a cadence that sways listless pines"

Quraysh Ali Lansana, born in Enid, Oklahoma, now lives in Chicago, Illinois.

Michael Madonick – In The Field

"When I exit my back door, which faces north, I can hear through the cornfield, to my right, the sad grinding mechanisms of Wall Street and the literati. To my left, over the soy beans, I register what sounds like the clanking of free-weights and the bloated cars of Beverly Hills' plastic surgeons. I know I live in the Midwest because I am curiously unimpressed by the impositions of the hyperbolic."

Michael Madonick was born in New York City, and now lives in Urbana, Illinois.

Stringtown Prison Poetry Workshop – The Stringtown Prison Blues

In the late 1970s, Mary McAnally led a poetry workshop for a small group of inmates at Stringtown Prison in Stringtown, Oklahoma. She taught at the prison twice a week, helping many of the prisoners get published in literary journals across the country. McAnally offered art as an alternative to violence. As she puts it, "You can murder someone in a poem and get away with it."

Wilma Elizabeth McDaniel – Spare Me Yellow Skies

Wilma Elizabeth McDaniel was born in Lincoln County, Oklahoma, thrown over to California with her family during the Dust Bowl and laid to rest in Tulare, California, after her death in 2007.

Jim Moore

"I know I'm in the middle of America when I'm walking along the Mississippi, which I do almost every day and in all weathers; the feeling of truly being betwixt and between thanks to the river; sunlight and shadow on water, no beginning and no end."

Jim Moore was born in Decatur, Illinois, and now lives in Minneapolis, Minnesota.

Ron Padgett – Driveway

Ron Padgett was born in Tulsa, Oklahoma, and now lives in New York City

Caleb Puckett – Karma, Oklahoma

"Red stems of pokeweed crowd the edges of the pasture. He drapes himself over the gate, pondering the hazards involved with having a salad with his steak."

Caleb Puckett was born in Albuquerque, New Mexico, and now lives in Ottawa, Kansas.

Sun Yung Shin – FOX FACE, SNOW FACE

"I know we're in the middle of America because the legacies and ongoing realities of conquest are everywhere—especially in what is now Minnesota, in which treaties (coinciding with the collapse of the European fur trade) were signed legalizing the land cessions by Dakota and Ojibwe people. Against these and other types of privatization, commodification, and violence, I see myriad forms of resistance: art, literature, community, civil disobedience, teaching, imagination, beauty, and rebuilding."

Sun Yung Shin was born in Seoul, South Korea, and now lives in Apple Valley, Minnesota.

Jeffrey Skemp – The Ease of Trout

"I'm in the Driftless Zone and our farm in the valley looks clean and lush, freshly cut windrows an x-ray of what's holding us up. But when the rain stops and the heat is relentless, our machines can barely leave a track; and so we bathe in cool water when we can as we mutter sweet distracted things to the ones we love, our fingers crossed."

Jeffrey Skemp was born in La Crosse, Wisconsin, and now lives in Minneapolis, Minnesota.

Joel Stein – Though a Country

"When I travel back to the Midwest or the Rocky Mountain West from the East Coast, I am immediately struck by the great dimensions, the endless sky and horizons in the interior of America. I feel as if I have stepped out of an enclosed room into a vast field of light and wind and sky. I feel as if I can breathe again and move without hindrance. I feel as if I have returned to where I began."

Joel Stein was born in Colorado and grew up in Ohio. He now lives in New York.

Odalee Still – timing

"I went to New York City once. Lost my voice in the horns and the rails and the concrete. But I found it. It was stretching into the middle, into this open blue, green, red land. This country can smell like pig shit, ozone, grass. Sweat, natural gas. There's a bunch of people in between here, America, and there, America. There's a man and a woman. There's a me and a you. And there's no telling what we'll do."

Odalee Still was born in Warren, Arkansas, and lives in Victoria, Texas.

Richard Stull – The 500

"When I visit my small hometown in Ohio, which I do several times a year, I am awash in the distant past and the people who populate it. My time there with its childhood hangover is infused with a poignancy equal to that nailed to the knowledge that I could never live there or probably anywhere in the Midwest again. The reasons are numerous. Despite our differences, the place and its inhabitants, living and dead, are the air I breathe."

Richard Stull was born in Mount Gilead, Ohio, and now lives in the Catskill Mountains.

Roy Turner – Hard Luck Okie

Roy Turner left Oklahoma City, Oklahoma, during the Great Depression and the Dust Bowl and began walking west in search of work. He recorded "Hard Luck Okie" for the Library of Congress at a migrant farmer's camp in California in the late 1930s.

Nick Weaver – The Orange Grove Is Beautiful This Time Of Year:

"Middle America is being trapped in the suburbs and seeking escapism through far-away college applications. You feel like you're suffocating in your hometown, but maybe someday you'll come back just to see what became of it."

Nick Weaver was born in Tulsa, Oklahoma, where he lives.

Michael White – Recurrence

"I grew up in Columbia, Missouri. Like so many Midwestern boys before me, I joined the Navy straight out of high school... I didn't even realize this was a cliché."

Michael White lives in Salt Lake City, Utah.

Jack Wendle – Ascension

"At an advanced age,
Knowing where in the hell you're at . . .
What was the question?

Happily married.
On my own I often smell
Others? Forbidden.

When Karen is gone
I spend my time abusing
the other senses."

Jack Wendle was born in Warren, Ohio, and now spends half of his time on Nettles Island and half in Youngstown, Ohio.

Kevin Young – Ode to the Midwest

Kevin Young was born in Lincoln, Nebraska, and now lives in Atlanta, Georgia.

Acknowledgements

My thanks go firs[t to everyone who contribu]ted original work to this anthology and the [poets (in *italics in This Land*)] who said "yes," when I asked them to rea[d their work into] my microphone. This project exists because of their voices.

There's a very special recording (wear headphones!) of the poem "EMPTY NEXT SYNDROME" by Paula Cisewski, which you can listen to at www.thislandpress.com/p2p. Thank you to Danielle Oberloier for driving to Tulsa from Oklahoma City to take part in that poetry experiment, James Johnson and Cedrick for lending their everything (especially their ears), post production associate engineer, Joshua Morales, for cleaning up our act and everyone at The Church Studio for lending me her space and slippery hardwood floors. Thanks to my dad for finding voice in the haiku. And to my mom for putting up with us poets!

Scott Gregory, thank you for your work as the poetry editor of This [Land and] for your encouragement and support on this [anthology, Vincent] Spears for bugging poets, Cecilia Whitehurst [for whipping my wor]k into shape, Kate Barron-Alicante and Steve [Cluck for their h]elp recording and editing and Jeremy Luther and [Zack Reeves for ma]king it look good.

Michael. Thank you for asking me, "what else?" I'd say the question's not so much "what" as "how?" And that's an endless thing.

Thanks for permission from the following publishers:

"Autobiography" was reprinted from *Collected Writings of Joe Brainard*, edited by Ron Padgett, with an introduction by Paul Auster (The Library of America, 2012).

"FALLING AND RISING" was reprinted from *Sea of Faith* (University of Wisconsin Press, 2004).

"Hardluck Okie" was reprinted from The Charles L. Todd and Robert Sonkin Migrant Worker Collection, Library of Congress, American Folklife Center. Additional archival voices on tape in this podcast are experts from oral histories from Dust, Drought and Dreams Gone Dry: Oklahoma Women in the Dust Bowl Oral History Project, courtesy of the Oklahoma

Oral History Research Program, Oklahoma State University Library.

"Spare Me Yellow Skies" was printed with permission from Back40 Publishing, 2009.

"The Stringtown Prison Blues" was reprinted from *Warning Hitch Hikers May Be Escaping Convicts* (Moonlight Publications, 1980).

P.S. — (Scott Gregory would like to express thanks to Michael Mason and Mark Brown at This Land Press, who both provided editorial guidance in the form of trust, insight, and feedback. Their commitment to running actual poems in This Land — recently written poems, no less, by living, breathing writers near and far — was and remains sincerely appreciated. Thanks also to the poets Quraysh Ali Lansana and John Brehm, each of whom did a poetry reading here in Tulsa, Oklahoma, that was sponsored by This Land — and each of whom thereby added distinction and direction to our cause.)